FUN
AROUND THE
WORLD

GAMES, CRAFTS, FOOD, AND DRESS IDEAS YOU CAN USE!

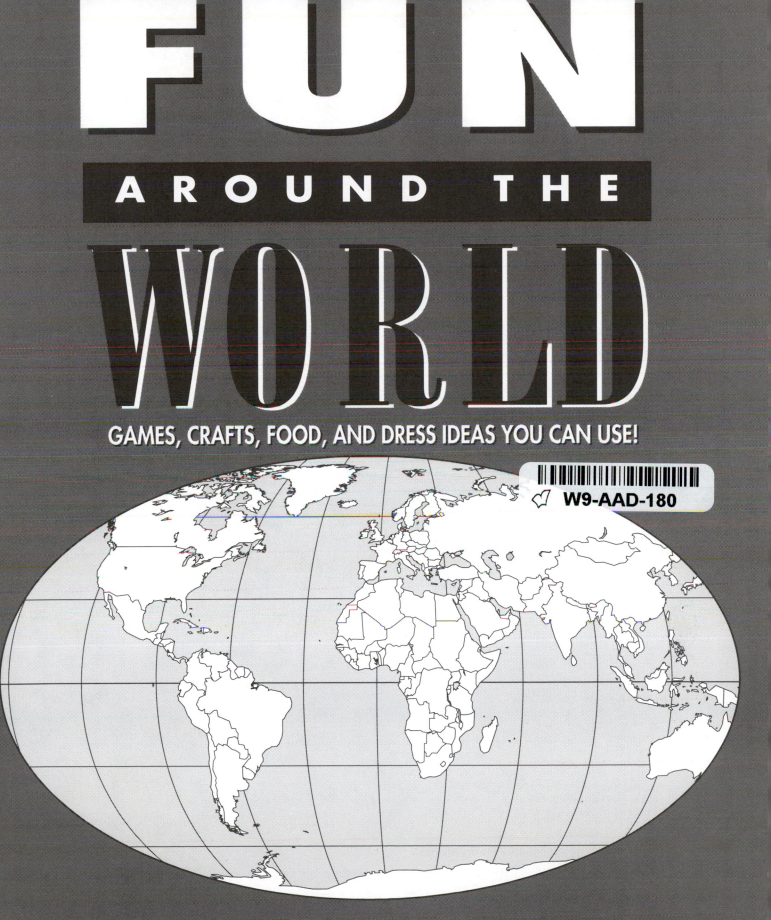

MARY BRANSON

New Hope
P.O. Box 12065
Birmingham, Alabama 35202-2065

© 1992 by New Hope
All rights reserved
First printing 1992
Printed in the United States of America

Dewey Decimal classification: 394
    GAMES, INTERNATIONAL
    COOKERY, INTERNATIONAL
    SONGS

Cover design from an oil painting by Mark Smothers
Illustrations by Susan Meyer

ISBN: 1-56309-052-X
N927103 • 0396 • 3M3

CONTENTS

ABOUT THE AUTHOR

Mary Kinney Branson has been writing children's materials for more than 20 years. Other books by Branson include *Adventures in Prayer*, *A Carousel of Countries*, and *It's Not Easy Being Small*. She lives in Atlanta, Georgia.

DEDICATION

We work best when we're encouraged by those we love. My special thanks to my greatest encourager—my husband—to whom this book is lovingly dedicated.

Song of Solomon 8:7

INTRODUCTION

The United States is like a colorful patchwork quilt. If each quilt block represents a different culture or language, the quilt has more than 500 blocks. That's how many culture groups our nation contains!

Each block is like all the others because people are people—no matter what their skin color or language. They laugh when something is funny; they cry when someone hurts their feelings.

Each block is different, too. That is what makes the quilt so beautiful. People of different languages and cultures look and dress differently; they enjoy different games, foods, and entertainment.

All the countries represented in this book have people living in the United States. Some shared their favorite ideas to help you understand their cultures.

Thanks to the following people for their contributions.

Roula Athan, member, Greek Gospel Church, Newton, Massachusetts

John Hionides, pastor, Greek Gospel Church, Newton, Massachusetts

Jimmy Kappas, member, Greek Gospel Church, Newton, Massachusetts

Roula Kappas, member, Greek Gospel Church, Newton, Massachusetts

Yoshiyuki Kawata, member, Kaumana Drive Baptist Church, Hilo, Hawaii

Soula Lykourgos, member, Greek Gospel Church, Newton, Massachusetts

Al Pecheco, catalytic home missionary, and Millie Pacheco, bilingual public school teacher, Windham, Connecticut

Merry Purvis, executive assistant, Church Extension Division, Home Mission Board, Atlanta, Georgia

Jack Roddy, Scripture Distribution, Home Mission Board, Atlanta, Georgia

Oscar I. Romo, director, Language Church Extension Division, Home Mission Board, Atlanta, Georgia

Hisayo Kathy Uchino, member, First Baptist Church, Westminster, California

Germany

Schultute [shool-too-tuh]

German parents give their children a treat called *schultute* to help them look forward to the first day of school. Some parents buy them in stores. Others make their own. Some *schultutes* are two-feet tall.

What you need:

10-inch square piece of poster board or very stiff paper; crayons or markers; masking or packing tape; candy; gum; small toys

What you do:

1. Draw a curved line from one corner to the opposite corner of the poster board (see illustration).
2. Cut the poster board on the line you drew.
3. Use crayons or markers to decorate the poster board.
4. Roll the poster board until the two straight edges overlap one inch, forming a cone.
5. Tape the sides together.
6. Fill the cone with candy, gum, and toys.

WORLD

Iran
Marbling

Marbling paper as an art form has been used in Iran for 500 years. The beginning and ending pages of books are sometimes marbled to add to their beauty. Use your marbled paper as wrapping paper or as a cover for one of your favorite books.

What you need:

old, square cake pan; enough water to fill the pan 1-inch full; 2 envelopes unflavored gelatin; 2 or 3 colors oil paint; paint thinner; stick or plastic knife; white paper, such as typing paper, cut to fit inside the cake pan; old newspapers

What you do:

1. Spread newspapers over the work area.
2. Pour the water in the pan. Add gelatin. Stir until dissolved.
3. Mix a little paint thinner with each color paint.
4. Drop a little of each color paint on the water. (The paint should float on top of the water.)
5. Stir the paint gently with the stick until the colors are swirled.
6. Lay a piece of white paper carefully on top of the water, then lift it off gently.
7. Drain the paper on the newspaper.

Japan
Bonsai

The Japanese art of growing tiny trees is called *bonsai*. Many Japanese families have *bonsai* trees that are more than 100 years old, and the trees are still small enough to fit in flower pots.

What you need:

small, clay flower pot; tree seedling (pine, maple, oak, etc.); potting soil; thin wire; wire cutters

What you do:

1. Pinch off the larger branches of the seedling.
2. Put the soil in the pot.
3. Plant the seedling in the soil.
4. Cut small pieces of wire. Wrap the wire around the branches, bending them in different directions. Attach the ends of the wire to the trunk of the seedling.
5. To care for your *bonsai*: Water often and keep in a sunny place. Pinch off branches as they grow. Continue guiding the directions the branches grow by bending them with wire.

Brazil
Terrariums

A terrarium can remind you of the many jungles and forests in Brazil. Brazil has the largest rain forest in the world. Its jungles are filled with flowers, birds, and butterflies of every color.

What you need:

wide-mouth glass jar with lid; enough small stones or charcoal to cover the bottom of the jar; 1 to 2 cups potting soil; small plants or ferns (buy them, transplant them from your yard, or grow them from seeds); 2 to 3 small plastic or paper flowers, birds, or butterflies

What you do:

1. Put the stones in the bottom of the jar.
2. Put the soil on top of the stones.
3. Carefully place the plants in the soil, and pat the soil gently around them.
4. Arrange the plastic or paper items on the soil.
5. To care for your terrarium: Water your plants only when they seem dry. Keep the lid on the jar except when a lot of moisture collects on the sides of the jar; then remove the lid for a day. Trim the plants with scissors, or pinch off long leaves when they grow too tall.

Iran
Mosaic Container

A mosaic is made of colored fragments such as glass, tiles, or paper. Many walls, windows, and roofs in Iran's palaces are covered with mosaics. Even some streets are paved with mosaic glass and tile.

What you need:

small can (such as lemonade mix or coffee can) with lid; white glue; 3 colors of powdered tempera paint; stick or plastic spoon; waxed paper; 3 squeeze bottles like those used for mustard and catsup

What you do:

1. Pour white glue into the squeeze bottles.
2. Add a different color tempera paint to the glue in each bottle. Stir thoroughly. Put the lids on the bottles.
3. Squeeze small circles of colored glue onto the waxed paper. Let the circles dry completely.
4. Remove the circles from the waxed paper.
5. Use white glue to stick the circles to the sides and top of the can.
6. Use your mosaic container to store crayons or cookies. Or use it as a bank to save for a missions offering.

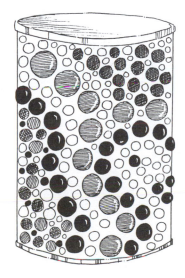

France
Pointillism

Pointillism artists place tiny dots of basic colors so close together that they appear to blend: blue and yellow become green; red and yellow become orange. Pointillism artists work many months to complete their paintings.

What you need:

hole punch; white paper; red, yellow, and blue construction paper scraps; pencil; white glue

What you do:

1. Punch lots of small circles from the construction paper scraps. Keep the colors separate.
2. On the white paper, draw a large outline of an orange with one or two leaves.
3. Glue a mixture of red and yellow circles on the orange shape.
4. Glue a mixture of blue and yellow circles on the leaf shapes.
5. Display your pointillism and step back at least ten feet. Do the red and yellow dots look orange? Do the blue and yellow dots look green?

Nigeria
Necklaces

Nigerian people enjoy wearing necklaces, earrings, wrist bracelets, and ankle bracelets. Sometimes they wear several necklaces at the same time. They make many of their beads from chunks of a gourd-like plant called calabash.

What you need:

16-inch piece of yarn for each child; yarn needle for each child (or wrap cellophane tape around the end of each piece of yarn so it will thread easily); lots of leftover buttons, all sizes and colors; wooden beads; paper towels; white glue; marking pens; pencils

What you do:

1. Tear the paper towels into small pieces.
2. Dip each piece in white glue.
3. Shape the paper towel pieces into balls around a pencil. While the paper towel balls are still wet, gently slide out the pencil.
4. Allow the paper balls to dry. Each ball should have a hole completely through the center.
5. Decorate the balls with marking pens.
6. String the balls on the yarn, mixing them with buttons, and wooden beads.
7. Tie the ends of the yarn together.

Japan

Origami

The art of paper folding is called origami. Japanese children and grown-ups enjoy origami. They use special paper in bright colors and metallic coatings to create airplanes, animals, birds, houses—almost every shape.

What you need:

a 6-inch square of lightweight paper for each child

What you do:

1. Fold the paper in half to form a triangle (see illustration).
2. Fold the triangle twice for smaller triangles.
3. Fold the end triangles behind the front ones.
4. Fold the tips of the back triangles.
5. Fold the bottom of all four triangles so the shape's bottom section will rest on a flat surface and the paper shape will stand.
6. Draw a face on the front of the paper shape. You have folded paper to look like an animal's head.

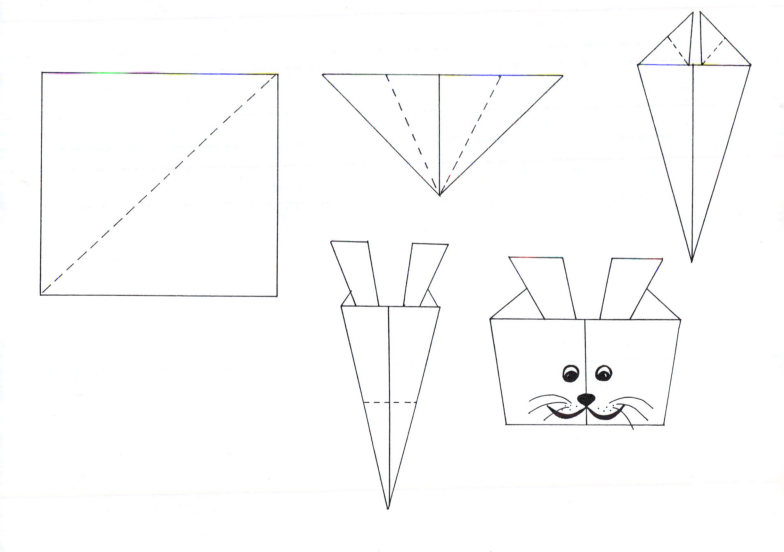

11

America
Indian Buzz Toys

American Indians make buzz toys from pieces of gourds, shells, leather, wood, and twine. By twisting and pulling on the twine, you can make the object spin. If you pull the twine tight, relax it, then pull it tight again, the toy will make a buzzing sound.

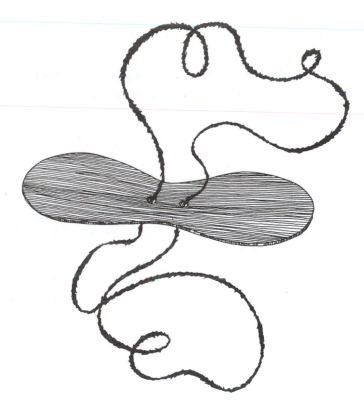

What you need:
1½-by-3-inch piece of gourd, shell, leather, wood, or other hard material; 3 feet heavy twine; hand or electric drill; sandpaper

What you do:
1. Use the sandpaper to smooth any rough edges on the material.
2. An adult should drill two holes in the middle of the object (see illustration).
3. Thread the twine through the holes.
4. Tie the ends of the twine together.

Poland
Paper Cutouts

Wycinanka Ludowa [vee-tchee-nahn-kah Loo-doh-vah] is the name of folk paper cutouts made by Polish people. Long ago they cut the paper designs only at Easter. They would hang the paper cutouts on the walls of their homes until the next Easter. Now, people in Poland make the paper designs at Christmas and throughout the year. They also make greeting cards using the cutouts.

What you need:
4-by-5-inch piece of thin colored paper, such as wrapping paper; small scissors; white glue; 1 sheet construction paper; marking pen

What you do:
1. Fold the thin paper in half, then fold it in half again. While it is folded, cut small portions from the paper. Unfold the paper.
2. Fold the construction paper in half to make a 4½-by-6-inch card. Glue the paper cutout to the front of the card.
3. Write a message on the inside of the card. Give your card to a friend.

Switzerland
Egg Decorating

At Easter, Swiss people make beautifully decorated eggs using small leaves. Brown onion skins are used to dye the white eggs brown. Tiny green leaves make white prints on the egg. Swiss girls and boys play egg-cracking games with hard-boiled eggs. They search for eggs with pointed ends for the contest. Children who can dent others' eggs without cracking their own, win the contest.

What you need:
uncooked white egg; 2 or 3 tiny leaves, such as parsley; 10-inch piece of old pantyhose; brown outer layers of an onion; 6-inch piece of string; small pot of water; stove or hot plate

What you do:
1. Wet the leaves just enough to make them stick to the egg. With the leaves sticking to the egg, wrap the pantyhose around the egg. Tie the ends tightly with the string.
2. Place the egg in the pot of water. Add the onion layers. Bring the water to a boil, then reduce heat and simmer 15 to 20 minutes.
3. Pour out the water. Remove the pantyhose and leaves from the egg. Run cold water over the egg.

Spain
Lanterns

Some Spanish families make lanterns which are sold all over the world. Similar lanterns have been used for 200 years in Spain.

What you need:
empty aluminum can with the top removed; hammer; nail; permanent marker; 12-inch piece of wire; old newspaper; small candle; masking tape; match

What you do:
1. Shred newspaper and pack it in the can until the can is filled tightly. Place the masking tape across the top of the can to keep the paper from falling out.
2. Use the marker to draw a design on the can.
3. Place the can on several layers of newspaper. Use the nail to hammer two holes near the top of the can, across from each other. Pull the wire through the holes. Twist the ends of the wire to form a hanger.
4. Hammer holes on the lines of the design. Remove the masking tape and newspaper.
5. Light the candle. Drip candle wax into the bottom of the can. Blow out the candle. Place the candle in the wax while the wax is still hot. Do not move the can or candle until the wax has dried completely.
6. Turn the can on its side to light the candle. Then hang the can or place it on a table.

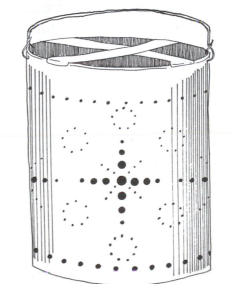

Haiti
Aluminum Sculptures

Haitians make and sell aluminum sculptures.

What you need:
disposable aluminum pie pan or broiler pan; permanent marking pen; scissors or tin shears; hammer; nail; newspapers

What you do:
1. Use the marking pen to draw a simple picture on the bottom of the pie pan. Draw the details of the picture with the marking pen, too. Use the scissors or tin shears to cut out the picture.
2. Place the picture on the newspapers.
3. Use the hammer and nail to punch lots of holes along the lines of the picture. Use the hammer to smooth rough edges made by the nail.

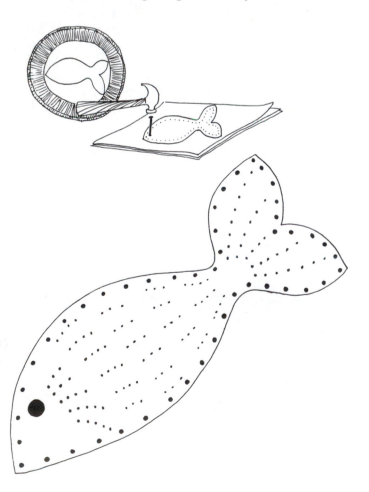

Greece
Embroidery

Embroidery is popular in Greece, but it's difficult for children to do. Boys and girls begin learning to embroider in school by using this simple method.

What you need:
9-by-12-inch piece of poster board for each child; marker, crayon, or pencil; straight pin; embroidery needle; yarn

What you do:
1. Draw a simple picture on the poster board: a flower, an animal, a piece of fruit.
2. Use a straight pin to punch holes every ¼-inch along the lines of the drawing.
3. Thread a piece of yarn on the needle.
4. Weave the yarn in and out of the holes. When you run out of yarn, leave the end of the yarn on the back of the picture. Thread another piece of yarn and continue weaving.
5. Continue until the entire picture is outlined.

Ghana
Woven Belts

People in Ghana make belts, clothing, and blankets by weaving materials together. Women weave wide belts more than a foot wide. Men weave narrow belts about six inches wide. Sometimes strips of weaving are sewn together to make blankets and clothing.

What you need:
4 plastic straws; yarn in several bright colors

What you do:
1. Cut four pieces of yarn, 70 to 80 inches long.
2. Cut ½-inch from one of the straws. Thread one piece of yarn through the small piece of straw. Pull the straw to the middle of the yarn.
3. Push the two ends of the piece of yarn through the long piece of straw.
4. Prepare the other three straws and pieces of yarn the same way.
5. Tie all the ends of the yarn together in a tight knot, with two inches of loose yarn on one side of the knot.
6. Tie the end of a yarn strand to one of the straws.
7. Holding the four straws together, weave the yarn over and under the straws. When you get to the last straw, weave in the opposite direction.
8. Continue weaving around the straws. If you get to the end of a yarn strand, tie another strand of yarn to it.
9. When you have woven two or three inches on the straws, push the woven yarn off the straws and onto the loose yarn.
10. Keep weaving and pushing the yarn off the straws until the woven part is long enough to go around your waist.
11. Cut off the small pieces of straws. Pull the longer straws off the yarn. Tie this end of the yarn in a tight knot. Cut the loose yarn to two inches to match the other end.

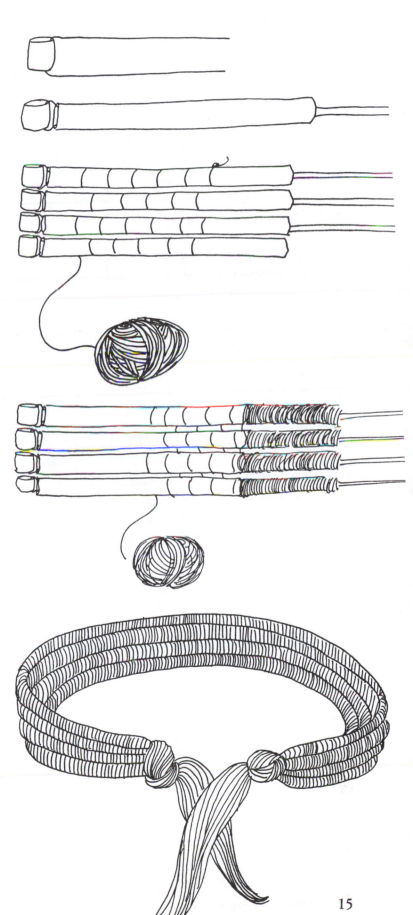

New Year's Day Celebrations

People find it exciting to end an old year and start a new year. New Year's Day celebrations have been going on about as long as there have been people to celebrate.

In ITALY children receive small gifts of money on New Year's Day. In Rome, Italy, people give gifts to the traffic officers. In GREECE, children are awakened at midnight to welcome the new year and open gifts. In FRANCE, people stay up until midnight and give New Year's Day kisses under the mistletoe. In SCOTLAND, people share Hogmanay shortbread (recipe on page 37) and wassail (fruit punch) to celebrate the new year. In IRAN, people celebrate *Noruz* [NO-rooz]—Iranian New Day. Their *Noruz* celebration starts March 21 and lasts 12 days. Iranian children receive gifts and new clothes during *Noruz* celebrations. Friends exchange gifts of colored eggs, fruit, and flowers. On the last day of *Noruz*, families welcome spring by picnicking in the country.

In JAPAN, people celebrate *Oshoogatsu* [oh-show-GAH-tsu]—Japanese New Year. They clean their houses before the holiday. They decorate their houses with pine branches, bamboo stalks, and *shimekazari* [shee-may-KAH-zah-ree]. *Shimekazari* is a cluster of straw with seaweed, ferns, a red-and-white paper fan, and an orange or lobster attached. Japanese adults stay up to hear the new year welcomed in with 108 rings of a big gong. Children receive gifts, and everyone eats rice cakes.

In CHINA people celebrate *Yuan Tan* [WAHN-tah]—Chinese New Year. They remember everyone's birthday. Everyone agrees to forgive those they have been angry with. Children receive coins wrapped in red paper. The Chinese celebration lasts ten days. Friends exchange gifts of nuts and tea. Houses are decorated with flowers and red candles. There is a parade on the last day.

What you can do:

Give a New Year's Day gift to a police officer, teacher, or church helper. Make Hogmanay shortbread and wassail. Color eggs and give them to friends; have an Iranian New Day picnic.

Sing "Happy Birthday" to everyone, make friends with anyone you've been angry with, and have a Chinese New Year's Day parade.

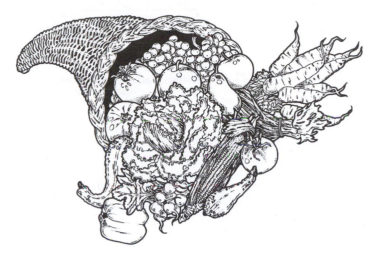

Thanksgiving

People have thanked God for their good harvests for hundreds of years. Thanksgiving began for Christians in Europe during the Middle Ages. A kind, Christian man named Martin, from Tours, FRANCE, was buried on November 11, A.D. 397. This date became the day when many European countries thanked God for His blessings. They called the celebration Martinmas, after Martin of Tours.

People of SWEDEN celebrated by cooking and eating goose. Children from GERMANY and the NETHERLANDS paraded with lanterns made of scooped-out pumpkins and gourds. Swiss children made lights from turnips. They called their lights *rabenlichters* [RAA-bin-lighters]. They hung them on sticks and carried them in parades through their villages.

In ENGLAND, farmers made dolls from ears of corn. They called the dolls "kern babies." Long ago the holiday was called Harvest Home in England. Farmers brought their extra vegetables, fruits, and flowers to the needy. Children wrote letters to neighbors who were old and poor. They put the letters inside baskets of food for their neighbors. As the children delivered the baskets of food, they learned to be thankful and to share.

When pilgrims came from England to AMERICA, they were used to thanking God for good harvests. After their first harvest in 1621, Governor William Bradford declared that the pilgrims would celebrate Thanksgiving, just as they had done in England. But the first American Thanksgiving meant more to the pilgrims than their English celebration. Besides thanking God for their harvest, they thanked Him for their new friends, the Indians. They invited Chief Massasoit and 90 of his braves to their Thanksgiving feast. The Indians brought five deer as gifts for the pilgrims. The pilgrims brought wild turkeys. The Indians and pilgrims celebrated for three days. They played games, held races, and sang songs.

What you can do:

Make a lantern from a gourd, pumpkin, or turnip. Prepare a food basket for a needy family and place handmade cards inside the basket.

THE WORLD

Poland
Hospitality

Most Polish people love guests—even uninvited guests! In Poland, not everyone has a telephone, so guests often show up unexpectedly. And they're usually welcomed warmly.

Most Polish people love food, so guests can expect lots of delicious food when they visit. Surprise guests will probably receive at least tea and pastries—cookies, pie, or cake. Invited guests may receive seven or eight delicious foods.

One Polish saying is *smacznego* [smatch-NAY-go]. It means "have a tasty meal." Another Polish saying is *gosc w dom, Bog w dom.* It means "a guest in the home is God in the home." Polish people believe they can serve God by being kind and loving to their guests. Read 1 Peter 4:9. Do you agree?

What you can do:
Use the recipes in this book to plan a delicious snack or meal. Invite a guest to share your food. How about inviting an older person who lives alone, your pastor, or a preschooler?

Japan
Hina-Matsuri

Hina-Matsuri is the Girls' Doll Festival. It is celebrated on March 3. Girls display their doll collections on shelves in their homes. Many dolls are dressed in costumes worn in Japan many years ago. Some dolls are dressed to look like Japanese rulers called emperors and empresses.

On *Hina-Matsuri*, girls take their dolls to friends' homes. They compare dolls and admire each others' doll collections. They give each other gifts of small cakes.

What you can do:
Choose your favorite dolls to display on a shelf. Visit girlfriends, compare dolls, and exchange cupcakes.

Japan
Tango-no Sekku

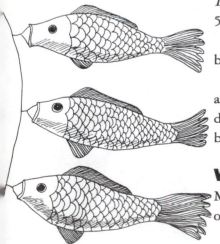

Tango-no Sekku [tahn-goh-noh sek-koo] is a holiday for boys. It is celebrated on May 5. Families hang carp-shaped flags outside their homes for each boy who lives there.

Carp are fish that Japanese people consider brave and strong. Parents hope their boys will grow up to be brave and strong, too.

In recent years, *Tango-no Sekku* has changed to *Kodomo-no-Hi*, or Children's Day, and includes girls. Japanese families still hang carp flags for their sons, but all children are honored. The holiday is a time to teach children the importance of being brave, strong citizens.

What you can do:
Make a paper or cloth carp-flag for each boy in your family or group. Hang the flags outside your house or room. Talk about ways girls and boys can be good citizens.

Thailand
Loy Krathong

Loy means *float*, and *Krathong* means *leaf*. Loy Krathong has been celebrated in Thailand for more than 600 years, but no one knows the exact reason for the holiday.

Loy Krathong is celebrated in November. Children cut banana leaves into all sorts of shapes, fold them, and fasten the ends with pins to form boats. They decorate their boats with flowers.

On the night *Loy Krathong* is celebrated, the children place small candles and coins in their boats and place the boats in rivers. The Thai rivers sparkle and glisten with thousands of candles. Grown-ups and children laugh and talk as they watch the boats float away. Fireworks explode in the dark sky.

What you can do:

Make a boat from cornhusks or a large tree leaf. Place a small, flat tea candle in the center of the boat. Take the boat outside near a lake or river. At evening, light the candle and place the boat in the water.

If you do not live near a lake or river, fill a large bucket or tub with water. Wait until evening, light the candle, turn out the lights, and place the boat in the water.

Africa
Storytelling

Most African children do not have television, movies, or amusement parks. They make their own fun.

Almost every evening, children and adults gather around a fire. Adults gather in a circle. Drummers sit behind them. Children sit on the sides.

Adults tell folk stories—stories they heard from their fathers, and their fathers heard from their grandfathers. The stories include acting, music, sound effects, and drums. The storytellers begin with riddles to teach girls and boys to notice things around them.

Then come the stories. The first stories are simple, and are usually told by young children. They are stories the children have heard many times. They are stories that teach lessons or explain why things happen, such as why the rooster crows.

Then teenagers and adults tell stories. These are exciting stories about brave, smart, or skillful people. They are stories that teach the children the history of their tribes.

What you can do:

Gather in a circle to tell stories. If possible, have a cookout at night. Start by asking riddles such as, "In winter, I am hard. In summer, I like to run" (ice/water).

Then ask younger children to tell Bible stories that teach important lessons, such as the boy who shared his lunch with Jesus. Or they may tell Bible stories that explain why things happen, such as the story of how God made the world. Finally, let older children or grown-ups tell stories of Bible heroes such as Mary, Martha, and Lazarus; Zacchaeus; Abraham; Jacob and Esau. Act out one of the stories. Sing a song that tells a Bible story.

Sweden

Pask Ris [POOSHK-rees]

Pask Ris means "Easter Twigs," and it's a holiday to welcome spring. Sweden's climate is cold and dark most of the year. People are anxious to welcome warm weather. They try to hurry the warmer season by bringing tree branches inside and putting them in water. They tie bright chicken feathers to the branches. Inside the warm houses, the branches sprout leaves much faster than the trees outside. The green leaves and colorful feathers make everyone feel that it's spring.

On April 30, Swedish people feel that spring has arrived. They sing songs of celebration around bonfires. The fires seem to chase away the dark, cold winter.

What you can do:

Bring a tree branch inside and place it in water. Decorate the branch with feathers or bits of construction paper. When buds appear on the branch, plan a celebration with spring songs and perhaps a cookout.

Switzerland

Sechselaeuten [SEK-se-loy-tin]

After many long, cold, and snowy winter months, Swiss children and adults are anxious to welcome spring. They do so with *Sechselaeuten*, celebrated on the third Sunday and Monday in April. *Sechselaeuten* means "six o'clock bells." The bells of a large church in the city of Zurich rang many years ago to announce the beginning of spring.

Today's celebration begins on Sunday with a children's parade. Children five-years-old and older dress in costumes and march through their towns and villages. On Monday, townspeople dress in historical costumes that represent their jobs. They join the children in another parade. A dummy of a snowman—made of white cotton—waits at the end of the parade. The snowman is filled with firecrackers and sits on a pile of branches and logs. The snowman's name is *Boogg* [beuk], which means "Old Man Winter."

When the *Sechselaeuten*—six o'clock bells—begin ringing, a fire is lit under the snowman. The fire burns brightly, the firecrackers explode, and the children celebrate the end of Old Man Winter and the beginning of spring.

What you can do:

Celebrate the beginning of spring by making a snowman dummy from a white shirt, white pants, white cotton cloth, hat, scarf, and gloves. Have a parade. Ring a bell, and let the snowman, *Boogg*, join the parade. Or plan a cookout and ask each child to make a snowman from three marshmallows. Marshmallow snowmen can be toasted and eaten.

Hanukkah is the Jewish Festival of Lights. The celebration lasts eight days, and helps Jews remember when God made a tiny bit of lamp oil keep the light in the Temple burning for eight days.

Jewish families light candles each night during Hanukkah. The candlestick, which holds eight candles, is called a menorah. The first night, families light one candle; the second night, they light two. They light one more candle each night until, on the last night of Hanukkah, the entire menorah is lit. After lighting the candles each night, families thank God for His care.

Jewish children receive gifts each night during Hanukkah. They sing special songs and everyone plays with a spinning top called a dreidel.

Hanukkah is celebrated at different times during the winter because Jewish people use a different calendar—a moon calendar—to determine its date. Hanukkah is often celebrated in December.

What you can do:

Make a dreidel (page 54).

CHRIST'

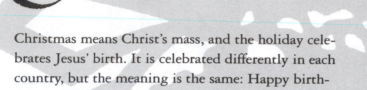

Feliz Navidad   クリスマス
             おめでとう

Christmas means Christ's mass, and the holiday celebrates Jesus' birth. It is celebrated differently in each country, but the meaning is the same: Happy birthday, Jesus!

In FRANCE, boys and girls find small toys in their shoes on Christmas morning, but in SWITZERLAND, children have a parade to celebrate the holiday.

In SWEDEN, people enjoy a Christmas Eve feast. Swedish families bake lots of cakes and cookies at Christmas. They make their cookies in shapes that remind them of Jesus: cross, star, church door.

SWEDISH, DANISH, and NORWEGIAN children feed wild birds at Christmastime. Swedish children tie a large stalk of grain to a pole. Norwegian children shape animal fat (suet) and bird seed into blocks, tie the blocks onto sticks, and place them in the snow.

In AUSTRIA, children decorate Christmas trees with nuts wrapped in silver or gold foil.

In DENMARK, families go to church on Christmas Eve. Then they enjoy a feast of rice pudding and goose. One almond is hidden in the pudding. Whoever finds it receives a candy pig called a *marzipangris*. After supper, the children see the Christmas tree for the first time. It is decorated by the adults.

In MEXICO Christmas is celebrated for nine days. Each celebration begins with a parade and a *posada* [poh-SAH-dah] party. *Posada* is Spanish for "inn," and each party starts with a parade where people act out the story of Mary and Joseph searching for a place to stay while Jesus is being born.

The parade moves from house to house (or from room to room within a house). Two children lead the parade. They carry a tray with clay figures of Mary and Joseph, or pull the figures in a wagon. Other children follow them, carrying lighted candles. They knock at nine doors and ask, "Is there room at the inn?" Innkeepers open each of the first eight doors and tell them there is no room. At the ninth door, the innkeeper lets them in.

The last door opens into a nativity scene. The clay figures of Mary and Joseph, which the children have carried in the parade, are placed in the nativity scene. A figure of Baby Jesus, which is also carried in the parade, is placed in the nativity scene.

Each parade ends with a *posada* party and a piñata—a clay or papier-mâché container filled with treats. The piñatas are broken by the children. The last piñata is broken on Christmas Eve.

Some countries celebrate the 12th day of Christmas to remember that Jesus was baptized in the Jordan River and to remember that wise men visited Jesus when He was a boy. They call this day Twelfth Night, Epiphany, and Three Kings' Day. Gifts are often exchanged.

In SWEDEN, SWITZERLAND, and AUSTRIA, three children dress like wise men and others join them to parade through the streets singing Christmas carols.

FRENCH and ENGLISH children wonder each year who will be King or Queen of the Bean during Epiphany. Grown-ups place a bean inside a cake before baking it. Whoever finds the bean in his or her piece of cake is given a gold paper crown and becomes King or Queen of the Bean for the next 12 days. If a girl finds the bean, she chooses a king. If a boy finds the bean, he chooses a queen.

TMAS
CELEBRATIONS

Joyeux Nöel

God Jul

Buon Natale

Fröhliche Weihnachten

What you can do:

- Have a parade to celebrate Jesus' birth.
- Bake cookies in shapes that remind you of Christmas.
- Make a bird feeder.
- Make Austrian tree decorations.
- Make a pudding, and hide an almond inside. Plan a prize for the person who finds the almond.
- Plan a Mexican Christmas parade and posada party. Make clay figures of Mary, Joseph, and Jesus. Make a Christmas piñata by filling a paper sack with candy and small toys. Decorate the sack with markers or crayons. Tie the end of the sack tightly with heavy twine and tie the twine to a ceiling. Take turns blindfolding your friends and letting them try to break the piñata with a broom handle. When the piñata breaks, share the treats.
- Celebrate the 12th day of Christmas by reading the stories of the wise men and Jesus' baptism.
- Make a bean cake: Prepare a cake mix according to package directions. Pour the batter into the cake pan. Before baking, add a large, dried lima bean or a shelled almond. Stir, then bake. Plan a small surprise for the person who finds the bean.

Vietnam

Tet Trung-Thu

Tet Trung-Thu is the biggest holiday of the year for Vietnamese children. *Tet Trung-Thu* means "Mid-Autumn Festival." It is celebrated in September or October. People celebrate by giving moon cakes to friends and family. Moon cakes are rice cakes filled with peanuts, raisins, and other treats. The cakes are placed in decorated boxes.

    Tet Trung-Thu began with the legend of Emperor Minh-Hoang, who lived in the eighth century. In mid-autumn, the emperor was supposed to have read a poem to his empress, Duong-Quy-Pho, by the light of the full moon. The moon cakes remind people of this story.

    Before *Tet Trung-Thu*, children make all kinds of lanterns. On the night of the celebration, they put candles in their lanterns. They march through the streets to the music of drums and cymbals.

What you can do:

Make a moon cake by spreading peanut butter on a rice cake. Add raisins and more peanut butter. Top with another rice cake. Wrap the moon cake in plastic wrap. Tie the wrap with a bright ribbon. Give the cake to someone special.

Israel

Rosh Hashanah

Rosh Hashanah means "Head of the Year" and is the Jewish New Year, which is celebrated in autumn. Jewish people spend extra time in prayer during Rosh Hashanah. Jewish people believe that God created the world at this time of year, so Jewish children sing "Happy Birthday, World" during their celebration.

Rosh Hashanah is also known as *Yom Teruah*—the Day of the Blowing of the Ram's Horn. A ram's horn, or *shofar*, reminds Jewish people that God calls His people to live better lives.

Jewish people eat special foods on Rosh Hashanah: apple slices and honey, honey cake, and *challah* (a round or braided bread). They also eat fruits that ripen in autumn, and *tzimmes* [TSIM-mes]—a baked dish that contains sweet potatoes, meat, prunes, and carrots.

Many Jewish people send cards to friends and family on Rosh Hashanah.

What you can do: Make "Happy Birthday, World" cards for family and friends. Spend time in prayer and thank God for creating the world. Plan a way to make the world around you better by picking up litter, recycling cans, or planting a tree or flower.

25

SONGS AROUND THE W

Brazil

Recording Bird Calls

Several years ago, the most popular song in Brazil was a recording of the song of the tiny *viro puro* bird. The reason for its popularity was that many people did not believe the *viro puro* bird existed. Most people could not hear its song because it lived deep in the jungle.

Finally a German ornithologist—someone who studies birds—traveled deep into the Brazilian jungle. He recorded the *viro puro* from far away so he wouldn't scare it. Then he played his recording loudly. The *viro puro* thought the recording was another bird and flew closer. The ornithologist was able to make a better recording.

What you can do:

Take a tape recorder to a quiet place. Record a bird call. Then play the recording loud. Maybe another bird will answer.

26

ORLD

Israel

Singing Scriptures

Jewish people have set Bible verses and Bible stories to music for hundreds of years. It's a great way to learn memory verses.

What you can do:

Sing a Bible verse to a familiar tune. Or make up a tune for a Bible verse using a piano, zither, xylophone, or melody bells to choose the notes.

"JESUS LOVES ME"

Sing the familiar tune to the chorus of "Jesus Loves Me."

Africa
- Use these Swahili pronunciations.
  Yay-soo ah-nee pen-da
  Yah-soo ah-nee pen-da
  Yah-soo ah-nee pen-da
  Bee-blee-ah ah-nee say mah

France
- Use these French pronunciations.
  Wee, Zhay-zuee meh-mer
  Wee, Zhay-zuee meh-mer
  Wee, Zhay-zuee meh-mer
  La Bee-bler dee teh-se

Arabic Countries
- Use these Arabic pronunciations.
  The aa sounds like the a in cat.
  Kahd faa-kah hub-nah
  Kahd faa-kah hub-nah
  Kahd faa-kah nub-nah
  Yu-hib-bu-nah Yah-so

Japan
- Use these Japanese pronunciations.
  Wah-gah Shoo Yay-soo
  Wah-gah Shoo Yah-soo
  Way-gah Shoo Yah-soo
  Way-ray oh ah-ee-soo

Russia
- Use these Russian pronunciations.
  Lyoo-beet Ee-ee-soos
  Lyoo-beet Ee-ee-soos
  Lyoo-beet Ee-ee-soos
  E-to tvyer-do snah-yoo yah

"HOW GREAT THOU ART"

Sing the familiar tune to the chorus of "How Great Thou Art."

Hungary

• Use these Hungarian pronunciations.

See-vehm feh-layd, ooy-yohng er-rerm-tah-lay
  Meely nady vady Tay
  Meely nady vady Tay
See-vehm feh-layd, ooy-yohng er-rerm-tah-lay
  Meely nady vady Tay
  Meely nady vady Tay

"I HAVE DECIDED TO FOLLOW JESUS"

Sing the familiar tune to the chorus of "I Have Decided to Follow Jesus."

Alaska (the Eskimo Indians)

• Use these Eskimo pronunciations.

Owl-lah-nik-tuu-nga maleeng-nyah-jee-
  gah Jesus
Owl-lah-nik-tuu-nga maleeng-nyah-jee-
  gah Jesus
Owl-lah-nik-tuu-nga maleeng-nyah-jee-
  gah Jesus
Oo-tee joo-mee-nyeyt nga
Oo-tee joo-mee nyeyt ngah

India

• Use these Hindi pronunciations.

Yee-soo kay pee-chay meh chull-nay luh-
  gah
Yee-soo kay pee-chay meh chull-nay luh-
  gah
Yee-soo kay pee-chay meh chull-nay luh-
  gah
Nuh low-doo-gah, nuh law-doo-gah

"HE LEADETH ME"

Sing the familiar tune to the chorus of "He Leadeth Me."

Greece

• Use these Greek pronunciations.

Meh oh-thee-yee, meh oh-thee-yee
Tee too hee-ree meh o-thee-yee
Ah-koh-loo-thee-soh tohn pis-tohss
Yah-tee tee hee-ree moh-thee-yee

Foods
World

Lebanon
Atayef Mehshi
Delicious stuffed pancakes
that people in Lebanon make.

Lebanon

Atayef Mehshi

What you need:
pancake mix, prepared according to
    package directions for 8 to 10
pancakes

2 cups chopped nuts

¼-cup sugar

1 tablespoon cinnamon

maple or corn syrup for topping

vegetable oil for frying

What you do:
1. Combine the nuts, sugar, and
   cinnamon. Set aside.
2. Cover the bottom of an electric
   skillet or frying pan with oil.
   Heat at medium, or 340°F,
   until the oil is hot.
3. Pour ¼-cup batter onto the hot
   oil. When the pancake starts to
   bubble, place two or three
   tablespoons of the nut mixture
   in the center.
4. Use a spatula to fold the pancake in half. Push the ends
   together with the spatula to seal
   in the nuts.
5. Continue cooking the pancake
   until it is light brown.
6. Cook the rest of the pancakes
   the same way. Serve them warm
   with syrup.

Japan

Mochi Cake

A Japanese treat that looks and tastes a lot like rice-cereal treats.

What you need:

1 stick and 1 teaspoon margarine, softened

1 cup sugar

1¼ cups milk

2 eggs

2 cups sweet rice flour

1 teaspoon baking powder

1 cup coconut

What you do:

1. Heat oven to 350°F.
2. Use an electric mixer to combine the margarine and sugar.
3. Add the milk and eggs.
4. Mix the flour, baking powder, and coconut. Stir them into the first mixture.
5. Rub the teaspoon of margarine on the bottom and sides of a 9-inch square baking pan.
6. Pour mixture into the pan. Bake for 40 minutes.
7. Cut into squares when cool.

Greece

Koulourakia

Cookie twists. They're a delicious Greek treat.

What you need:

4 cups all-purpose flour

1 teaspoon baking powder

¼-teaspoon baking soda

1 cup unsalted margarine

1½ cups sugar

1 whole egg and 3 extra egg yolks

2 tablespoons grated lemon or orange rind

1 teaspoon vanilla

½-cup plain yogurt

enough margarine to cover a cookie sheet

2 teaspoons water

What you do:

1. Heat oven to 375°F.
2. Mix the flour, baking powder, and baking soda together.
3. Use a mixer to beat the margarine and sugar until blended.
4. Add 1 egg, 2 egg yolks, the lemon or orange rind, and the vanilla to the margarine-sugar mixture. Beat until blended completely.
5. Gradually stir in the flour and yogurt. As you add more flour and yogurt, the mixture will become very thick. Use your hands to mix it.
6. If the mixture sticks to your hands after all the ingredients have been added, add a little more flour and mix it again.
7. Roll a handful of the mixture into a ball. Lay it on a piece of waxed paper. Use your hands or a rolling pin to roll the mixture into a long rope shape about as thick as your finger.
8. Cut the rope into pieces about 5 inches long. Twist each 5-inch piece into a loop (see illustration).
9. Rub a little margarine on a cookie sheet. Place the loops on the cookie sheet.
10. Mix the last egg yolk with 2 teaspoons of water. Brush this mixture on top of each loop. Bake for 15 minutes or until lightly browned.

Poland

Carrot-Spice Cake

If you are a guest in a Polish home, you will probably enjoy this or another delicious dessert.

What you need:

1 spice cake mix, prepared according to package directions

1 can cream cheese frosting

5 large carrots, grated

1¼ cups fruit preserves

¼-cup orange or lemon juice

What you do:

1. Add the carrots to the prepared cake mix.
2. Bake as directed on the cake mix package, using two 9-inch, round cake pans.
3. Mix the preserves and juice.
4. After they are completely cool, remove the cake layers from the pans.
5. Spread half the preserves on one cake layer. Place the other layer on top.
6. Frost the sides of the cake with the cream cheese frosting.
7. Spread the rest of the preserves on the top of the cake.

Greece

Greek Salad

What you need:

5 tablespoons olive oil

2 tablespoons vinegar

salt and pepper to taste

1 head iceberg lettuce

2 tomatoes

1 cucumber

1 green pepper

½-cup black olives

1 cup feta cheese

small amount of
   ground oregano

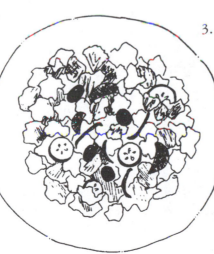

What you do:

1. Mix the olive oil, vinegar, salt, and pepper.
2. Tear the lettuce into bite-size pieces and place it in a large bowl.
3. Cut the tomatoes and cucumbers into bite-size pieces. Add them to the lettuce.
4. Cut the pepper in half. Scrape out the inside portion. Cut the pepper into thin slices. Arrange slices on top of the lettuce mixture.
5. Arrange olives on top of the lettuce mixture.
6. Crumble cheese on top of olives and peppers.
7. Sprinkle the oregano on top of the cheese.
8. Pour the oil and vinegar mixture on top.

Hawaii

Japanese Doughnuts

They were first made in Okinawa, Japan, but now they're a favorite of Hawaiian children.

What you need:

2 teaspoons baking powder

2½ cups plain flour

¾-cup sugar plus ?
 tablespoons

2 eggs

½-teaspoon salt

½-cup evaporated
 milk

2 tablespoons cooking oil

½-teaspoon vanilla extract

enough cooking oil to deep
 fry the mixture

paper towels

What you do:

1. Mix the flour and baking powder completely in a small bowl.
2. Mix eggs, sugar, milk, oil, salt, and vanilla in a large bowl. Stir until completely mixed.
3. Slowly add the flour mixture to the other ingredients. Mix thoroughly.
4. Heat the extra oil to 375°F in a deep fryer or electric skillet.
5. Drop mixture by spoonfuls into hot oil. Fry until light brown.
6. Drain on paper towels.

Puerto Rico

Puerto Rican Cookies

What you need:

3 cups flour

⅛-teaspoon salt

1 cup sugar

1 cup shortening or
 margarine

1 egg

1 teaspoon butter or
 margarine

What you do:

1. Heat oven to 350°F.
2. Mix flour and salt, set aside.
3. Beat the shortening until it is soft, then add the sugar a little at a time.
4. Add the egg and butter and mix well.
5. Blend flour into the shortening mixture.
6. Form small balls and press onto a cookie sheet.
7. Bake at 350° F for 10 minutes. After baking, the cookie may be decorated with a ¼ cherry or served as they are.

Frétourias day Kalabasa

Puerto Rico

Frituras de Calabazas

Pumpkin fritters are fried treats enjoyed by people in Puerto Rico.

What you need:

2 cups canned pumpkin

½-cup flour ¾ C

¼-teaspoon salt 2 TBL molasses

2 eggs

¼-teaspoon ground cloves

½-teaspoon ground cinnamon

2 ~~teaspoons~~ TBL sugar

cooking oil to fry the pumpkin mixture

paper towels

What you do:

1. Mix all the ingredients in a large bowl.
2. Heat the cooking oil to 375°F in a deep fryer or electric skillet.
3. Drop the pumpkin mixture by spoonfuls into the hot oil. Fry until golden brown.
4. Drain the pumpkin on paper towels. Serve warm.

Puerto Rico

Plantain Fritters

Tostones de platano verde may be served instead of bread or potatoes at a meal, or eaten like french fries for a snack.

What you need:

3 large green plantains (in the fruits section of the grocery—they look like green bananas)

1 teaspoon salt

medium-size bowl of water

enough cooking oil to deep fry the plantains

paper towels

waxed paper

What you do:

1. Use a knife to peel the plantains. Slice them in ¾-inch diagonal slices.
2. Put the salt in the water and stir.
3. Place the plantain slices in the water. Let them soak for 15 minutes.
4. Put the cooking oil in a deep fryer or electric skillet. Heat the oil to 375°F.
5. Take the plantain slices out of the water, but save the water.
6. Fry the slices in the oil. When the slices are golden brown, remove them from the oil.
7. Place the slices on waxed paper. Flatten them with a plate or the bottom of a large glass.
8. Dip the flattened slices in the water again.
9. Remove the slices from the water and fry them again in the oil.
10. Remove the slices from the oil, and drain them on paper towels.

Puerto Rico

Bacalaitos

Cod fish fritters are a favorite meal for many Puerto Ricans.

What you need:

½-pound dry, salted cod fish (fresh or canned)

2 cups flour

2 cups water

½-teaspoon salt

½-teaspoon baking powder

¼-teaspoon garlic powder

enough cooking oil to deep fry the fish

paper towels

What you do:

1. Place the fish in the water. Use your fingers to remove any pieces of bone or skin.
2. Let the fish soak in water for one or two hours.
3. Mix the flour with the baking powder.
4. Break the fish into small pieces and add the fish and water to the flour.
5. Use your hands to mix the fish and flour. Mix until all lumps are gone.
6. Add the salt and garlic. Mix again.
7. Place the cooking oil in a deep fryer or electric skillet. Heat the oil to 375°F.
8. When the oil is hot, drop spoonfuls of the fish mixture into it. Fry the fish until it is a light-brown color.
9. When it is fried, remove the fish. Drain each piece on paper towels.
10. Eat while warm.

Jamaica

Jamaican Casserole

What you need:

1-pound can of yams

1 banana

¼-cup orange juice

dash of salt

dash of pepper

¼-cup coconut

1 tablespoon margarine

What you do:

1. Heat an oven to 350°F.
2. Drain the liquid from the yams.
3. Slice the banana.
4. Spread the butter on the bottom and sides of a one-quart baking dish.
5. Put the yams in the dish.
6. Put the banana slices on top of the yams.
7. Pour the orange juice over the banana slices.
8. Sprinkle on the salt and pepper.
9. Sprinkle on the coconut.
10. Cover and bake for 30 minutes. Serve warm.

Scotland

Hogmanay Shortbread

A favorite treat for New Year's Day in Scotland.

What you need:

1 stick soft margarine

½-cup light brown sugar

2 cups sifted all-purpose flour

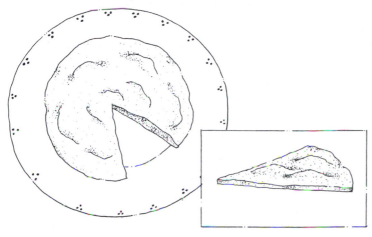

What you do:

1. Preheat oven to 350°F.
2. Use a spoon or your hands to mix the margarine and sugar.
3. Add the flour and mix with your hands. Mix just until blended.
4. Roll the mixture into a ball, and place it on an ungreased cookie sheet.
5. Press the dough with your hands until it is ½-to-¾-inch thick.
6. Bake until golden brown, 15 to 20 minutes.
7. Cool. Then use a spatula to remove the short-bread from the cookie sheet. Place it on a plate. Eat it right away, or cover tightly with plastic wrap. If eaten later, warm it in the oven or microwave.

Japan

Sushi

Japanese eat *sushi* on picnics, at parties, and as a snack. Hand-rolled *sushi*, called *temaki*, is assembled by the person who eats it. All the ingredients are placed on a table. Diners place the ingredients they want on sheets of *nori*, then fold the *nori* and eat. Adult *sushi* contains raw fish, raw clams, octopus, and other adventurous foods. This recipe is a child's version of *sushi*.

What you need:

1 cup short-grain rice (not quick-cooking)

1 tablespoon rice vinegar (or 1 teaspoon sugar and 1 tablespoon white vinegar)

1 ounce roasted nori sheets (in the gourmet section of the grocery or in an Oriental market)

1 package imitation crab meat

1 avocado

1 large pickle

soy sauce

What you do:

1. Cook the rice according to package directions.
2. When the rice cools, stir in the vinegar.
3. Fold a sheet of *nori* in half, then in half again. Open it. The folding should break it easily into four pieces.
4. On one piece of *nori* (¼-sheet), place a small amount of rice. Spread it flat with a fork.
5. Put a bite-size piece of imitation crab meat on top of the rice.
6. Chop a small amount of avocado and pickle on top of the crab.
7. Sprinkle on a few drops of soy sauce.
8. Wrap the *nori* around the crab mixture, and eat.

Germany

Stollen

German bread. The bread is folded in half to represent Baby Jesus wrapped in swaddling clothes. *Stollen* is often given as a gift to new parents or at Christmas.

What you need:

frozen bread dough for 1 loaf (in the frozen food
    section at the grocery)

1 cup candied pineapple, raisins, or a
    combination of the two

1 tablespoon sugar

¼-teaspoon ground cinnamon

2 tablespoons margarine

¼-cup powdered sugar

What you do:

1. Bring the bread dough to room temperature.
2. Mix the fruit into the bread by squeezing and punching the dough—it's called kneading.
3. Follow package directions for making the dough rise.
4. Place the risen dough on a floured surface. Press it into a 9-by-12-inch flattened piece.
5. Melt 1 tablespoon margarine. Brush on dough.
6. Mix cinnamon and sugar. Sprinkle over the margarine.
7. Fold the dough in half lengthwise, making a 4½-by-12-inch shape. Pinch the long edge to seal the dough.
8. Rub 1 tablespoon of margarine on a cookie sheet. Place the dough on the cookie sheet.
9. Cover the dough loosely with plastic wrap. Place it in a warm place until it doubles in size, about 1 hour.
10. While the dough is rising, heat the oven according to bread package directions.
11. Bake the bread until it is lightly browned.
12. Remove the bread from the cookie sheet while it is still warm. Let the dough cool completely. Then sprinkle with powdered sugar.

Cinnamon

Greece

Dolmas

(Greece and many Middle Eastern countries)
Stuffed grape leaves. They are delicious as a main
dish or appetizer.

What you need:

8-ounce jar of grape leaves, drained (in the
    gourmet section of the grocery or at a
    Middle Eastern grocery)
1 pound ground beef or
    lamb (or a
    combination)
2 cups cooked
    instant rice
2 cans condensed beef broth
¼-teaspoon garlic powder
¼-cup lemon juice
1 carton sour cream or plain yogurt

What you do:

1. Cook the meat in a microwave or frying pan.
   Drain off the fat.
2. Mix the meat with the rice, 1 can of beef broth,
   and the garlic.
3. Carefully drain the liquid from the grape leaves.
   Rinse them in cool water and drain them on
   paper towels with the shiny sides of the leaves
   facing down.
4. Place a spoonful of the meat mixture in the center of a leaf. Fold two opposite sides of the leaf
   toward each other. Then fold the
   other two sides toward each other.
   Fill each leaf the same way.
5. Place the leaves, seam sides
   down, in a pan.
6. Mix the lemon juice and 1 can beef broth. Pour
   this mixture over the leaves.
7. Bake at 350°F or microwave until heated thoroughly.
8. Spoon sour cream or yogurt on top of each, and
   serve warm.

Israel

Latkes

Jewish people eat these potato pancakes on holidays
such as Hanukkah.

What you need:

1 pound raw potatoes
¼-cup onion flakes
½-cup boiling water
2 small eggs
3 tablespoons
    flour
½-teaspoon salt
¼-teaspoon baking powder
dash of pepper
cooking oil for frying
small jar applesauce
paper towels

What you do:

1. Grate the potatoes on a hand grater or in a food
   processor. Set aside 1 cup grated potatoes.
2. Mix the onion with the rest of the grated potatoes in a large bowl.
3. Pour boiling water over the potatoes and onions.
4. Add the cup of potatoes you set aside, eggs,
   flour, salt, baking powder, and pepper. Blend all
   ingredients thoroughly.
5. Cover the bottom of a skillet
   with cooking oil. Heat to 360°F.
6. Drop spoonfuls of the potato
   mixture into the hot oil. When the
   mixture is light brown on the bottom, turn each
   mound over. Brown them on the other side.
7. Remove from the oil and drain on paper towels.
8. While still warm, spread applesauce over each
   potato mound. Serve immediately.

GAMES ... WO

Greece

Tob Mantilakee

"The hankie" is a game enjoyed by Greek children. Greek children also enjoy *skinakee* (jump rope) and *psilo keeneegeetoh*. *Psilo keeneegeetoh* is similar to tag, with rocks and stones serving as safe spots where children cannot be tagged.

What you need:

handkerchief; eight or more children

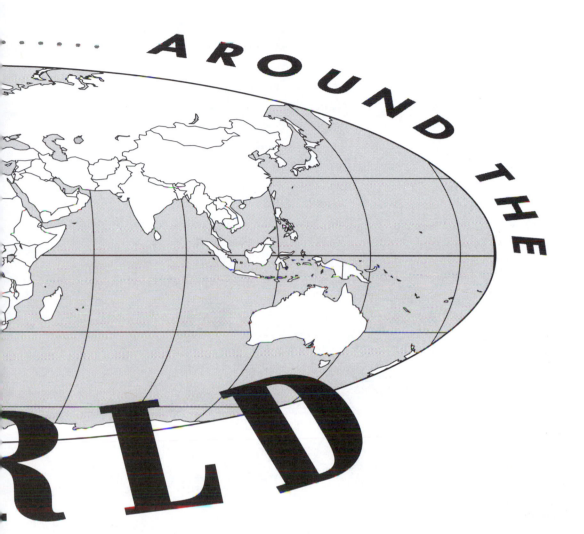

AROUND THE WORLD

What you do:

1. Divide the children into two teams. If there is an odd number of children, one child can hold the handkerchief. If there is an even number of children, an adult can hold the handkerchief.

2. Assign numbers to children on both teams. Each team should have a 1, a 2, a 3, and so on.

3. Have the teams form parallel lines about ten feet apart. Team members should line up in order of the numbers assigned with children standing in the opposite locations of the children with the same numbers:

Team 1	Team 2
1	4
2	3
3	2
4	1

How you play:

1. The leader stands between the two lines and holds the handkerchief by one corner.

2. The leader calls a number.

3. Both children with that number try to grab the handkerchief and return to their places without being tagged by the other.

4. Each time a child grabs the handkerchief and returns to his or her place without being tagged that child's team gets one point.

5. The team with the most points when time is called is the winning team.

Japan

Fruit Basket

A Japanese game much like musical chairs.

What you need:

one less chair than children playing

What you do:

1. Place the chairs in a circle.
2. Assign each child one of these fruits: apple, orange, banana, pear; repeating the fruits as much as necessary.
3. Choose a child to be "It" and stand in the center of the circle of chairs. Ask the other children to sit in the chairs.

How you play:

1. The child who is "It" calls out the name of one of the fruits assigned to the children. All children with that assignment stand and change seats. "It" tries to sit in one of the empty seats.
2. The child left without a seat gets one point. This child calls out another fruit and tries to find an empty seat.
3. The game continues in this way. Instead of naming a specific fruit, "It" can say, "fruit basket," and everyone must change seats.
4. When a child has three points, he or she is out of the game. Each time a child leaves the game, a chair should be removed.
5. Continue until one chair and two children remain. These children are declared the winners.

France

"My Great Aunt Lives in Tours"
A game played by French children.

My great-aunt lives in Tours...

What you need:
at least three children

What you do:
1. Seat the children in a circle.
2. Choose a child to start the game.

How you play:
1. The first child says, "My great aunt lives in Tours (a city in France) in a house with a cherry tree and a little mouse—squeak, squeak."
2. The child to the first child's right repeats what the first child said and adds the name of another animal and that animal's sound. For example: "My great aunt lives in Tours in a house with a cherry tree and a little mouse—squeak, squeak— and a red cow—moo, moo."
3. The third child repeats everything said so far and adds another animal and its sound.
4. The game continues until every child has added an animal. The first child must then repeat the entire description of the house in Tours.

Africa

Jarabadach

A game played by African children

What you need:

2 players; 3 small markers of one color and 3 of another color (or 3 pennies and 3 nickels); paper and pencil or a stick to draw in the sand or dirt

What you do:

1. Draw a square on paper or in sand or dirt.
2. Divide the square into four smaller squares

How you play:

1. Give one player the three markers of one color; give the other player the other markers.
2. Players take turns placing their markers on any of the nine points of the square. They try to place their three markers in a row or diagonally.
3. After all six markers are placed on points of the square, players take turns moving markers, one space at a time, until one player gets his or her markers in a row. That player is the winner.

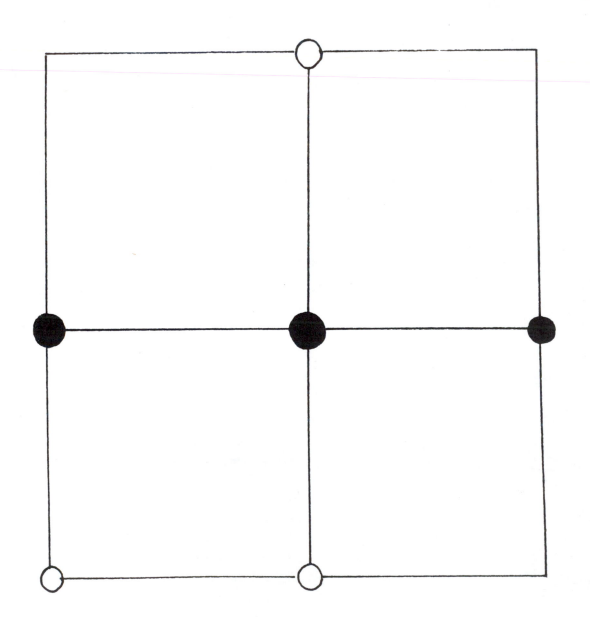

Philippines

Stoop Tag

A favorite game of Filipino children

What you need:

at least 3 children

What you do:

Choose a player to be "It."

How you play:

1. The player designated as "It" chases the other players. If a player is tagged, he or she becomes another "It," and both "Its" chase the others.
2. A player may escape being tagged by stooping, but each player may only stoop three times.
3. The game continues until all players have been tagged. As the game progresses, more and more children will be "Its," so the game becomes more difficult for those children not yet tagged.

Italy

Morra

A game played by Italian children. It's a good way for younger children to practice adding numbers.

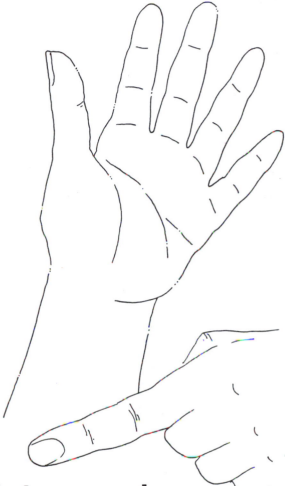

What you need:

at least 2 players

What you do:

Divide the players into teams of two.

How you play:

1. The leader counts aloud to three.
2. On the count of three, each player on each team extends one to five fingers of his or her hand. Immediately after counting, the leader calls out a number between two and ten.
3. If the fingers extended by a team of players totals the number called by the leader, that team gets one point.
4. The team with the most points when time is called is the winning team.

Cuba

Spain and Cuba

Cuban children play this form of tag.

What you need:

6 or more children

What you do:

1. Divide the children into two groups. Designate one group as Cuba and the other as Spain.
2. Place the groups in parallel lines at least ten feet apart.

How you play:

1. Select a player from the Spain side to cross to the Cuba side.
2. All players on the Cuba side stand with one hand extended, palm up.
3. The player from Spain walks by each player, rubbing his or her hand across each player's open palm.
4. Instead of rubbing one Cuba player's palm, the player from Spain slaps the palm and runs back toward the Spain side. The player whose palm was slapped runs after the Spain player. If the Cuba player tags the Spain player before he or she reaches the Spain side, the Spain player must join the Cuba side, and a Cuba player goes to the Spain side and selects a player for the chase.
5. If the Spain player returns to his or her side without being tagged, another Spain player crosses to the Cuba side and the game continues.
6. The game continues until all players are on one side or time is called.

China

Stir-Fry Turnover

Chinese children play this game which is similar to the American game Fruit Basket Turnover.

What you need:

a chair for all players except one

What you do:

1. Place the chairs in a circle, with a child sitting in each chair. The extra player, "It," stands outside the circle.

2. Children are assigned names of fruits and vegetables. Use American fruits and vegetables, but also try these Chinese ones: bamboo shoots, water chestnuts, and litchi nuts. If the group is large, make a list of the names assigned so "It" will remember to call on each child.

How you play:

1. "It" calls the names of two fruits and/or vegetables. The children with these assignments exchange seats. While they are scrambling to change seats, "It" tries to sit in an empty chair. If "It" is successful, the child without a chair becomes "It."

2. "It" may also call, "Stir-fry turnover," and all children must change seats.

3. The game continues until time is called.

China

Chinese Pick-up Race

Chinese children use marbles, but beginning chopstick users will find marshmallows or popcorn easier.

What you need:

2 small bowls, such as cereal bowls, for each player; 1 pair of chopsticks or two plastic drinking straws for each player; 5 miniature marshmallows (or pieces of popcorn) for each player

What you do:

1. Place half the bowls at one end of the room and half at the other end.
2. Place five marshmallows in each bowl at one end of the room.

How you play:

1. Each player stands beside a bowl with marshmallows, holding the chopsticks in his or her hand.
2. When the leader gives the signal, each player uses chopsticks to pick up one marshmallow. It must be picked up with the chopsticks; fingers cannot touch it.
3. Players walk briskly (don't run) to the bowls on the opposite side of the room. If they drop their marshmallows, they must start again.
4. When players reach the bowls at the opposite side of the room, they place their marshmallows in the bowls and walk back to the first bowls.
5. Players continue until all marshmallows are transported to the opposite side of the room.
6. The first player to carry all his or her marshmallows is the winner.

Bolivia

Juego del Panuelo

The handkerchief game is a game played in Bolivia.

What you need:

handkerchief; chair for each child except 1; 12 or more children

What you do:

Place the chairs in the shape of an *x*, with four rows of chairs radiating from a central point like spokes.

How you play:

1. Choose one child to be "It." All other children sit in chairs.

2. "It" walks around the outside of the chair formation, carrying the handkerchief.

3. "It" drops the handkerchief behind one of the rows of chairs.

4. The children sitting in the row where the handkerchief is dropped get up, run completely around all four rows of chairs, and return to any seat in their row.

5. While the children are running, "It" sits in one of the empty chairs.

6. The last child to return to his or her row will be left with no chair. This child becomes "It," and the game continues.

7. Play long enough for each row to participate.

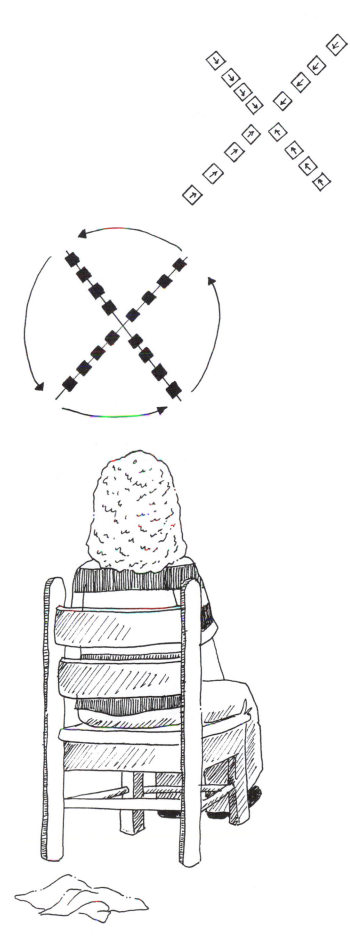

Alaska

Tug-of-War

A game played by Eskimos

What you need:

masking tape if the game is played indoors; 6 to 20 children

What you do:

1. Divide into two equal teams. If you have an uneven number, one player can signal when to start and judge which team wins.
2. If you are playing indoors, place a two-foot piece of masking tape on the floor to mark the crossover line.
3. If you are playing outdoors, use a tree or other object to mark the crossover line.

How you play:

1. Team members line up behind each other, with one team on each side of the crossover line.
2. Players at the fronts of the lines lock hands.
3. Team members wrap their arms around the waists of the members in front of them.
4. At the signal to start, each team tries to pull the other team over the line. The first team to pull the leader of the other team over the line wins.

England

Troy Town Mazes

English children make and exchange mazes. Many years ago, the mazes were made by digging paths in dirt or by marking lines with stones. Now children draw the mazes on paper.

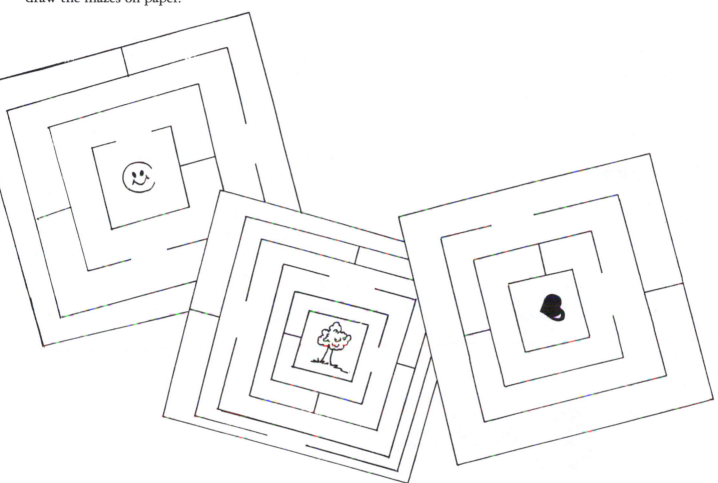

What you need:

paper; pencil; ruler for each child

What you do:

Each child should:

1. Draw an object in the center of a sheet of paper. The object could be a heart, a smiley face, a tree—anything.
2. Draw a square around the object, but leave part of the square undrawn. This makes a door to get to the object.
3. Draw a larger square around the first square, leaving another door. Anywhere within the space between the two squares, draw a line connecting the squares.
4. Add a third square, leaving a door and drawing a line connecting it to the second square.
5. Draw as many squares as you like. The more squares you draw, the harder it will be to get to the object.

How you play:

1. Trade papers with another child.
2. Use a pencil or your finger to trace a path from the outside door to the object inside the smallest square.

...ngland. Women in England dress in
...rves for this race. They race 415 yards,
toss... ...kes three times. Most racers finish in
about one minute.

What you need:

2 lightweight frying pans; permanent marking pens;
2 flexible toss toys, 2 large plastic lids, or two 8-inch
circles of poster board (whatever you choose should
fit easily inside the frying pans, and they should be
exactly alike); bell to ring

What you do:

1. Draw a large 1 on one side of the toy, lid, or
   poster board circle. Draw a large 2 on the other
   side.
2. Place these "pancakes" inside the frying pan.

How you play:

1. Divide players into two equal teams, with an
   additional player serving as bell ringer.
2. Mark a starting line and a finish line. The dis-
   tance between the lines will depend on the size
   of the play area.
3. Have players form two lines behind the starting
   line, with the players at the front holding the
   frying pans.
4. When the bell ringer rings the bell, the first
   player from each team runs from the starting line
   to the finish line and back to the starting line.
   While the players are running, they must flip
   their pancakes three times. They can see if the
   pancakes flip by checking the number that faces
   upward. Players should continue trying until
   they flip their pancakes successfully.
5. If a pancake falls to the ground, the player must
   go back to the starting line and begin again.
6. When players complete the race, they pass their
   frying pans to the next players, who continue the
   relay.
7. The first team with all players completing the
   race wins.

Africa

Oware or Mankala

This is called the Game of the Universe, or Star Play. It's a game played in many African countries. It has many names, and usually is played around noon when it's too hot to play active games.

What you need:

2 egg cartons; scissors; stapler or masking tape; 48 dried beans or seeds

What you do:

1. Cut the top from one egg carton.
2. Cut two sections from the other carton. Tape or staple one of these sections to each end of the first section.
3. A player owns the sections on his or her side and stores beans in the extra section to the right.
4. Place 4 beans in each of the 12 playing sections.
5. The first player picks up all the seeds from any section that belongs to him or her. She plants one seed into each of the next four consecutive cups. For example, if she chooses cup 2 she would then put one seed in 3, 4, 5, and 6. (Note: A player may never begin a move from the other player's row.)
6. The second player does likewise. For example, if she selects cup 10, she would place one seed in cups 11, 12, 1, and 2.
7. The game continues in this manner with each player moving all the seeds from the chosen cup and planting one in each consecutive cup. The object of the game is to capture as many seeds as possible from the opponent's cups. Seeds may be captured in two ways:
   - When your last seed planted lands in an opponent's cup already containing one or two seeds (and no more), you may capture these seeds.
   - Going backward from that last cup, you can collect seeds from all consecutive cups containing only two or three seeds.
8. The game ends when one player has 24 seeds in her "home cup" or when neither player has a move. At that point, the player with the most seeds wins.

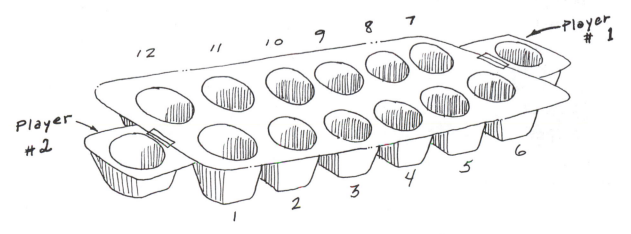

Israel

Dreidel Toy

Used by Jewish adults and children for hundreds of years.

What you need:

a round toothpick; a 2-inch square piece of poster board; a fine-tip marker

What you do:

1. Divide poster board into four equal triangles by drawing lines from corners to opposite corners.
2. Copy one of the following words or symbols in each triangle:

   nun

   gimel

   hay

   shin

3. Poke the toothpick through the center of the poster board where the lines cross.

How you play:

1. The words you wrote are Hebrew letters. They stand for *nes gadol hayeh sham*, which means "a great miracle happened there."
2. Hebrew letters stand for numbers, too, and you will need the numbers to play the game:

   nun=50
   gimel=3
   hay=5
   shin=300

3. Decide how long you want to play or decide on a number of points that must be earned to win.
4. Take turns spinning the top you made. Each player receives the number of points represented by the letter that is highest in the air when the top stops spinning.
5. The player who earns the winning number of points, or who has the most points when time is called, is the winner.

Israel

Dreidel Box

Dreidel boxes are used at holiday celebrations.

1. Each child takes a turn spinning the *dreidel* toy. He or she chooses a piece of yarn on the side marked with the same Hebrew letter the *dreidel* toy lands on. The child pulls the yarn until the toy comes out of the box.

2. The activity continues until every child gets a toy. If a child spins a letter where no yarn pieces are left, he or she spins again.

3. If you use funny sayings or Bible verses, ask children to read their sayings aloud.

What you need:

cardboard box (without lid) at least 1-foot square; marking pen; 3-foot piece of yarn for each child; small toy; piece of candy; joke, funny saying, or Bible verse (printed on a small piece of paper) for each child; a Jewish *dreidel* toy (see page 54)

What you do:

1. Print one of these Hebrew letters on each side of the box: nun, gimel, hay, shin. Or use the symbols:

   nun:

   gimel:

   hay:

   shin:

2. Tie a small toy or other object to the end of each piece of yarn.

3. Place the toys in the box, letting the yarn pieces hang over the sides of the box where they can be seen on the outside. Hang an equal number of yarn pieces over each side of the box.

4. Place the box high enough so the children cannot see inside.

Scotland

Kilts

Scottish Highland dancers wear plaid skirts called *kilts*. The hat is called a *tam-o'-shanter*. Highland dancers play bagpipes.

What you need:

short plaid skirt (even for boys!); 10-by-36-inch piece of plaid cloth or a plaid shaw; knee socks; beret or military hat; blazer or suit jacket; dark-colored swimming trunks; leather belt; small drawstring cloth purse; shirt or blouse

What you do:

1. Put on the swimming trunks, shirt, and socks.
2. Put the skirt on over the swimming trunks.
3. Pull the belt through the handles of the purse, and put on the belt. The purse will hang from the belt.
4. Put on the blazer and the hat.
5. Drape the plaid cloth over one shoulder.

Panama

Polleras

Panamanian women wear embroidered blouses and skirt outfits called *polleras* for special occasions.

What you need:

enough white cloth (an old sheet will do) to wrap around your waist and reach to the ground; safety pin; 2-by-4 foot piece of white cloth (cut from the same sheet); decorative pin; fine-tip marking pens; silk or paper flowers; hair pins; golden necklace with a medallion or brooch attached

What you do:

1. Use the markers to decorate both pieces of cloth. Make your designs look as much like embroidery as possible.
2. Wrap the larger piece of cloth around your waist and fasten it with the safety pin.
3. Wrap the smaller piece of cloth around your arms—like an off-the-shoulders blouse. Fasten it with the decorative pin.
4. Put on the necklace.
5. Fasten the flowers in your hair with the hairpins.

Japan

Kimonos

The *kimono*, Japan's native dress, is worn on special occasions such as New Year's Day and *Hina-matsuri*.

What you need:

For girls:

light-colored or flowered floor-length bathrobe; 3 feet of 12-inch cloth; flowers or bows for hair; sheet of construction paper; stickers of flowers or animals

For both:

rubber-sole thong shoes

For boys:

dark-colored floor-length bathrobe; 3 feet of 3-inch cloth; dark-colored short bathrobe or pajama top

What you do:

For girls:

1. Put on the bathrobe. Pull it as far around you as possible, closing up the space at the neck.
2. Use the wide cloth as a belt, tying it in back.
3. Place bows or flowers in your hair.
4. Put on the shoes.
5. Place the stickers on the construction paper. Fold construction paper back and forth to form a fan.

For boys:

1. Put on the long bathrobe. Pull it as far around you as possible, closing up the space at the neck.
2. Tie the cloth strip around your waist, fastening it in the back.
3. Put the short bathrobe on over the long one.
4. Put on the shoes.

Finland

Folk Costumes

What you need:

For girls:

floor-length skirt and vest (or floor-length jumper); apron; long-sleeved blouse with full sleeves; 2 scarves; 2 feet of gathered lace

For boys:

tight-fitting pants; high boots or knee socks; shirt; vest; short jacket; 2 feet of 1-inch ribbon; felt or leather hat with small brim

What you do:

For girls:

1. Put on the blouse.
2. Put on the shirt and vest or the jumper.
3. Tie the apron around your waist.
4. Wrap one scarf around your neck and tie it in front.
5. Wrap the other scarf around your head and tie it low in the back.
6. Wrap the lace around your head and tie it where you tied the scarf.

For boys:

1. Put on the shirt and pants.
2. Pull the boots or knee socks over the pants.
3. Tie the ribbon in a bow around your neck.
4. Put on the vest and jacket.
5. Put on the hat.

Greece

Greek Folk-dancing Costumes

People in Greece don't wear this sort of clothing everyday, but they dress in folk costumes for holidays and celebrations.

What you need:

For girls:

floor-length full skirt; long-sleeved blouse; large necklace; 2-foot ribbon (if your hair is long enough to braid)

For boys:

shirt with full, long sleeves; man's necktie; vest; short skirt; knee socks; two 24-inch pieces of 1-inch wide ribbon; tight-fitting knit cap; tassel from an old curtain tie (or made from yarn); safety pin

What you do:

For girls:

1. Put on the skirt, blouse, and necklace.
2. Tie or pin your hair back. If your hair is long enough, braid the ribbon into it.

For boys:

1. Put on the shirt and skirt.
2. Tie the necktie around your waist.
3. Put on the vest.
4. Put on the knee socks. Tie a ribbon at the top of each sock.
5. Use the safety pin to attach the tassel to the cap. Put on the cap.

Denmark

Folk-dancing Costumes

What you need:

For boys:

loose pants; knee socks; shirt; scarf; short jacket; stocking cap; two 2-by-3-inch pieces of yellow poster board; masking tape; black marking pen

For girls:

long skirt; blouse; apron; 2 scarves

What you do:

For boys:

1. Put on the pants and shirt. Put the knee socks over the pants.
2. Use the marking pen to darken the centers of the poster board pieces.
3. Roll pieces of masking tape and place two pieces on the back of each piece of poster board.
4. Press one piece of poster board against the front of each shoe (like buckles).
5. Put on the jacket and stocking cap.
6. Tie the scarf around your neck.

For girls:

1. Put on the skirt and blouse.
2. Tie the apron around your waist.
3. Tie one scarf around your neck.
4. Fasten the other scarf around your head, tying it in back.

Holland

Folk Costumes

Folk costumes worn in Marken, an area of Holland. Holland has many folk costumes. Most look like these.

What you need:

For girls:

long skirt; blouse; scarf; half-sheet poster board; close-fitting cap or shower cap

For boys:

baggy pants; knee socks; jacket; hat with a small brim

For both:

one sheet brown or yellow poster board; masking tape

What you do:

For girls:

1. Enlarge pattern A to cut a shape for the wings of the cap.
2. Place the cap on your head. Wrap the poster board wings around the cap and tape them together in the back.
3. Put on the skirt and blouse.
4. Tie the scarf around your neck.

For boys:

1. Put on the baggy pants.
2. Pull the knee socks over the pants.
3. Put on the jacket and hat.

For both:

1. Enlarge pattern B to cut four shapes from poster board.
2. Tape two shapes together to fit over a shoe. Tape the other two shapes together to fit over the other shoe.

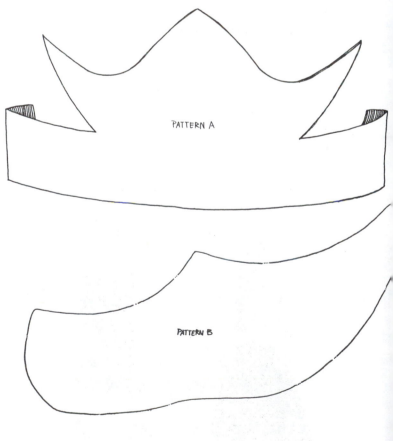

PATTERN A

PATTERN B

Alaska

Eskimo Clothing

The boots are called *mukluks*. They keep cold air out and body heat in.

What you need:

fur-lined parka with a hood; heavy pants; two 3-foot square pieces of dark cloth; two 3-foot pieces of rope or heavy twine

What you do:

1. Put on the pants.
2. Lay a piece of cloth on the ground. Place your foot in the center of the cloth. Pull up the cloth until it covers your foot.
3. While you hold the cloth around your foot, ask a friend to wrap the rope around your foot and ankle and tie it snugly at the top.
4. Put on the parka.

Iran

Iranian Wedding Dress

Her wedding day is one of the biggest days in an Iranian girl's life. She receives lots of gifts, including a large loaf of decorated bread—3 feet long and 1½ feet wide.

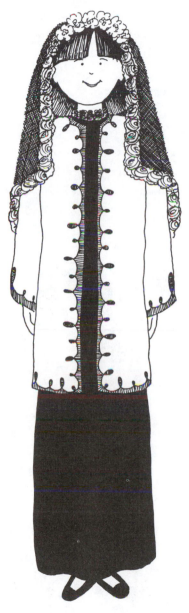

What you need:

long red dress; long coat or jacket (embroidered if possible); 2-by-4-foot piece of white veil or net; hair pins; 2 or 3 silk flowers

What you do:

1. Put on the dress and jacket.
2. Use hair pins to fasten the veil in your hair. Fasten the flowers where the veil meets your hair.

Nigeria

Agbadas

Most African clothing is loose-fitting, light-colored, and comfortable because of the heat. In Nigeria boys wear loose shirts called *agbadas*, loose-fitting pants, and white robes. Girls wear long wrap-around skirts called *lapas*, scoop necked blouses called *bubas*, sashes called *iboruns*, and head cloths called *ageles*. Everyone enjoys wearing brightly colored jewelry.

What you need:

For boys:

simple white shirt; pajama bottoms (blue, if possible—it's the favorite color of most Nigerians); white robe or oversized white shirt; several necklaces and bracelets made of wooden beads (see Necklaces, page 10)

For girls:

blouse with round neckline and no collar; piece of cloth wide enough to wrap easily around the waist and long enough to reach from the waist to the floor; piece of cloth 2-to 3-feet wide and long enough to tie under the arms; piece of cloth 1-foot wide and long enough to tie easily around the head, lots of brightly colored jewelry (see Necklaces, page 10)

What you do:

For boys:

1. Put on the shirt, pajama bottoms, and robe.
2. Put on the necklaces and bracelets.

For girls:

1. Put on the blouse.
2. Tie the first piece of cloth around your waist.
3. Wrap the second piece under your arms and tie it on the side.
4. Tie the third piece around your head.
5. Put on the jewelry.

Haiti

Clothing is simple because most Haitians are poor. Many women carry heavy objects on their heads, especially baskets of fruit. They do it so often that they become skilled at it. How far can you walk with the basket of fruit on your head?

What you need:

brightly colored dress—red, yellow, blue, pink, or green (flowers and prints are often used for Haitian clothing); white apron; flat straw basket; plastic fruit; wire, glue, or masking tape; several colorful bangle bracelets; 1½-by-4-foot piece of cloth

What you do:

1. Put on the dress.
2. Tie on the apron.
3. Fasten the fruit in the basket with the wire, glue, or tape.
4. Put on the bracelets.
5. Tie the cloth around your head so no hair shows. Tie the cloth in the back, at the neckline.
6. Balance the basket of fruit on your head.

BIBLIOGRAPHY

"A Country Celebration." *Family Circle*, December 1989.

Amari, Suad. *Cooking the Lebanese Way*. Minneapolis: Lerner Publications Company, 1986.

Baldwin, Gordon C. *Games of the American Indian*. New York: W. W. Norton & Company, Inc., 1969.

Blinn, Johna. *International Cookbook*. New York: Playmore, Inc., Publishers and Waldman Publishing Corp., 1989.

Caballero, Jane; Whordley, Derek. *Children Around the World*. Atlanta: Humanics Limited, 1983.

Chung, Okwha; Monroe, Judy. *Cooking the Korean Way*. Minneapolis: Lerner Publications Company, 1988.

Cole, Ann; Hass, Carolyn, et. al. *Children Are Children Are Children*. Boston: Little, Brown, & Co., 1978.

Collan, Anni; Heikel, Ynguar. *Dances of Finland*. New York: Chanticleer Press, 1948.

Crossfield, Domini. *Dances of Greece*. New York: Chanticleer Press, 1948.

Cummings, Richard. *101 Costumes for All Ages, All Occasions*. Boston: Plays, Inc., 1987.

Einhorn, Barbara. *West German Food and Drink*. New York: The Bookwright Press, 1989.

Harbin, E. O. *Games of Many Nations*. New York: Abingdon Press,1954.

Harrison, Supenn; Monroe, Judy. *Cooking the Thai Way*. Minneapolis: Lerner Publications Co., 1986.

Hart, Jane, compiler. *Singing Bee!* New York: Lothrop, Lee, and Shepherd Books, 1982.

Henry, Edna. *Native American Cookbook*. New York: Julian Messner, 1983.

LaFargue, Francoise. *French Food and Drink*. New York: The Bookwright Press, 1987.

Lorenzen, Poul; Jeppesen, Jeppe. *Dances of Denmark*. New York: Chanticleer Press, 1950.

MacFarlan, Allan *A. Book of American Indian Games*. New York: Association Press, 1958.

Merkel, Judi, Ed. *Home Cooking—Cook with the Best*. Berne, Ind.: The House of White Birches, 1990.

Merkel, Judi, Ed. *Home Cooking—Cooking with Style*. Berne, Ind.: The House of White Birches, 1990.

Merkel, Judi, Ed. *Home Cooking—For Cooks Who Care*. Berne, Ind.: The House of White Birches, 1990.

Nguyen, Chi; Monroe, Judy. *Cooking the Vietnamese Way*. Minneapolis: Lerner Publications Co., 1985.

Osborne, Christine. *Southeast Asia Food and Drink*. New York: The Bookwright Press, 1989.

Polon, Linda; Cantwell, Aileen. *The Whole Earth Holiday Book*. Glenview, Ill.: Scott, Foresman & Co., 1983.

Purdy, Susan. *Festivals for You to Celebrate*. Philadelphia: J. B. Lippincott Co., 1969.

Sandor, Haraszit. *Evangeliumi Enekek*. Atlanta: Home Mission Board, 1974.

Severson, Jilann. "Hanukkah." *Better Homes & Gardens*, December, 1990.

Streh, Judith. *Holiday Parties*. New York: Franklin Watts, 1985.

Temko, Florence. *Folk Crafts for World Friendship*. Garden City, N. Y.: Doubleday & Company, 1976.

Ven-Ten Bensel, E. Van. *Dances of the Netherlands*. New York: Chanticleer Press, 1949.

Warren, Lee. *The Theater of Africa*. Englewood Cliffs, N. J.: Prentice-Hall, Inc., 1975.

Zamojski-Hutchins, Danuta. *Cooking the Polish Way*. Minneapolis: Lerner Publications Company, 1984.

Zibell, Akugluk Wilfried, Ed. *Atuutit Mumiksat*. Atlanta: Home Mission Board, 1976.